Social Misfit

EKTA SOMERA

also by ekta somera

made in poetry
twenty-two

Social Misfit

EKTA SOMERA

ISBN 978-1-0370-6069-4

Printed in the Republic of South Africa

Copyright © Ekta Somera 2025

Cover illustration by Sonia Naidoo

All rights reserved. No part of this book may be reproduced in any form or by any electronic or mechanical means, including information storage and retrieval systems, without written permission from the author, except in the case of a reviewer, who may quote brief passages embodied in critical articles or in a review. The information in this book is distributed on an "as is" basis, without warranty. Although every precaution has been taken in the preparation of this work, neither the author nor the publisher shall have any liability to any person or entity with respect to any loss or damage caused or alleged to be caused directly or indirectly by the information contained in this book.

The universe wrote this poem for my heart
to keep beating, when I begged to make it stop.

"This is a book for anyone learning to live in their own shape. It offers no grand declarations, only the slow, brave work of naming one's experience and trusting that it has weight. In a world that too often rewards performance over presence, Social Misfit stands as a quiet act of self-trust."

– **Caitlin Anne Tallack** *(Author of A Birthday Card in May)*

"Ekta Somera is the Rupi Kaur of South Africa - but better. Her words don't just rest on the page, they float effortlessly into our minds, pierce our melanin-clad skin, and take root in our hearts."

– **Sonia Naidoo** *(Author of Traumata, The Seasons of Femininity)*

"This collection of poems is a searingly honest exploration of the human experience, laying bare the complexities of identity, trauma, and resilience with unflinching vulnerability."

– **Luleka Mhlanzi** *(Award-Winning Poet & Author of Confiscated Identity)*

"Ekta's writing is incredibly powerful and evocative, filled with raw emotion and a deep sense of introspection. The way she weaves together personal pain, societal judgment, and self-discovery is both moving and profound."

– **Krsna Priya Dasa** *(Lotus FM Radio Jockey & Miss India SA 2015)*

"Social Misfit is a triumphant and emotionally relatable journey that will speak to women in any stage of self-discovery."

– **Arini Vlotman** *(Contemporary Romance Author & Life Coach)*

"Vivid, relatable, and refreshingly honest! Social Misfit speaks the voices of "traditional vs modern" feels - shining a light on the fragile but feisty human condition. It is both reflective and inspiring, stirring your strengths and weaknesses toward a resounding hope."

– **Shika Budhoo** *(Actress, Writer, Author, Acting & Drama Coach)*

To those who are called sensitive
the tiger's heart does not make it less fierce

Contents

Part One
the rejection .... *Page 9*

Part Two
the acceptance .... *Page 55*

Part One
the rejection

Social Misfit

Social Misfit

Muddy footprints follow
the tiger with invisible stripes
shrugged away
with claws of contempt -
the untamed beast
still walks in fierce solitude
as a silent roar echoes
through the unseen path.

Social Misfit

There were holes in my heart
that I filled with people
who used subtle gestures
like wooden swords
to hurt me gently -
now there are splinters gnawing
against wounds that were healing.

Social Misfit

My love overflowed
in every mindful deed -
I treated them no less
from strangers to family
mistaking their pity
for kindness
realising too late -
I emptied my heart
and theirs was full of greed.

Social Misfit

I understand people who tell it like it is, who say what is on their mind, and are not afraid to be blunt or brutally honest. It can be really brave... but sometimes, it is also a dangerous thing to speak without thinking, and mistake that for the truth, because the tip of your tongue carries venom when the mind is not in sync.

Social Misfit

Sticks and stones
they hurt and disappear -
words strike through
my skin and bones
leaving behind wounds
that only appear
to be healing -
it seems strange
the whispers about pain -
all the days I felt something
but not once stronger.

Social Misfit

Despite all the pain
I felt happiness again
but it came at a price
I could not pay -
when they degraded me
for having less money.

Social Misfit

Laughter grits through my ears
but I hear their feelings -
it's just a joke
that is why
it crawls up my spine
and makes me feel funny

I am bandaged with scars
and wounded by reality -
words reach much deeper
than metal through my skin
they take stabs at my heart
and call me sensitive for bleeding.

Social Misfit

It was a night like any other
except not for me
I walked in who I used to be
and out a different person

What did I do wrong -
I loved them
why did they hurt me -
maybe I deserved it
was it something I said -
it can't be

These thoughts became a noose
I wore like a scarf around my neck
tugging tighter each day
until I reached out to ask
why -
please tell me why -

And in that moment
I stopped breathing -
the ring around my neck
became a mockery
as they blamed me
for my sensitivity
to the pain they caused

Their words cut so deeply
it makes me wonder -
the scars I wear
are they really my fault?

Social Misfit

That did not feel like a knife in my back, because I saw it coming. This was more like a chainsaw in my chest, and I do not know if I have the strength to make it stop hurting.

Social Misfit

As blood dripped from my back
you mimicked tears
only to rub salt in my wound.

manipulation

Social Misfit

I cried and I cried
as if my tears could release
the unbearable weight
of their words
plunging through my chest

I cried and I cried
until my eyes turned sore
and the pain smothered
my feelings into rage
beneath all the heartache.

Social Misfit

The world is cold
and you are bleeding
there is no time to heal
before the next battle -

Without any armour
you carry a broken sword
rinsed in tears
and stained with blood -
you are still a warrior
even when you weep.

Social Misfit

In their mind, they were just being honest and there is nothing wrong with being honest... except, there is. When your honesty becomes arrogance, it blurs the truth and turns into disrespect. There are many ways to express authenticity without being rude, and without degrading another human being.

Social Misfit

Their true intentions
were masked beneath
acts of kindness -
they cared
in the way wolves care
about sheep -
following the norm
with self-righteous beliefs
and contradicting
every word they preach.

Social Misfit

This is a solitary battle
and I lost my weapons
in the ongoing war.

Social Misfit

Peering at your life
from behind fences -
standing on tiptoes
mocking away
I wouldn't do that -
they say

Voices echo
without any sound -
expert opinions
like spit in the air -
mindless assumptions
without any ground

An abundance of time
wasted in idle -
looking and talking
desperate to see -
blinded by all
they could never be.

critics without credentials

Social Misfit

Who are they -
these people
you hear things from
you read about

Who are they -
the ones you talk about
they tell you this and that
but always seem to sell you short
who are they -
to steal your dreams
to speak of things
they are not experienced in

Who are they -
to plague your thoughts
with distorted memories
and superstitions -
ask yourself
who are they -
to forge your beliefs
into their opinion

Who are they -
and why should you
believe anything
they tell you.

Social Misfit

I tried to escape
every home
I have ever lived in -
my mind was confined
to the four walls
that caged me -
what makes a monster
a question we often ponder -
perhaps it is the rage
of wanting things to change.

Social Misfit

Months passed by
and I could not see the sun
although it was right above me.

Social Misfit

Rock bottom has an echo
you hear it on the way down
when your body is dragged
across the rubble
of your broken spirit -
the air chokes you
and you cannot scream -
the ghost of your last hope
takes your hand as you near
a labyrinth of the abyss
and in attempt to escape -
you learn how to survive.

Social Misfit

Voices echo around my head
dancing without any music -
they remind me and I wonder
what does it mean when people say
they miss being a child
without any worries in the world -
my mind is wounded
from experiences
that forced me to grow up
I have no memory of a childhood
in which I am not suffering -
happiness is fleeting
something I am incapable of feeling.

Social Misfit

My first steps
were on eggshells -
shrinking to grow
from a broken home
into burning houses
chased from one side
to be caged in another -
blamed for their mistake
in choosing each other -
I nearly believed I was the match
setting every place I lived on fire.

Social Misfit

Some wounds do not heal
embedded by our own bloodline
the skin cannot scab
when there is nothing to bleed.

generational trauma

Social Misfit

My parents did their best to raise me
because their lives were not easy
I deserved better as a child -
that was not my burden to carry
but it did not stop me
from growing into an adult
who is understanding -

There are people who tried
to use my past against me -
but they failed
because I understand
we are all experiencing life
for the first time -
and the least we can do
is be kind to each other.

breaking cycles

Social Misfit

I think back to a time
before the wonder
was lost inside of me -
when the clouds
looked like candy floss
and imagining the taste
made me happy -

The scent of reality
fills the air
and I stop thinking -
the clouds appear
to bring more rain
as I drown in sorrow -
will my childlike sense
ever find its way back to me?

Social Misfit

Yellow was my favourite colour
when drawing the sun
at the corner of a page -
until it stopped shining for me
and my crayons broke
scribbling to darken
the shade of blue I felt -
all my friends drew rainbows
and colour filled their lives
as they found their pots of gold -
my tears mixed the yellow with blue
and everything turned green.

Social Misfit

The soft hum of angels singing
sounds like a high-pitched scream
to those raised on survival

Anxiety looms in the calm
as our mind prepares
to navigate the moment
it becomes chaos

The irony is -
despite the anticipation for disaster
we survive on hope that it won't last forever.

Social Misfit

I built castles in the air
with my head stuck in the clouds
now I am drenched in the rain -
wishing on stars I cannot even see.

Social Misfit

I wonder
if the butterflies remember
who they were
before earning their wings -

I wonder
if they mock the caterpillars
who cannot fly -
the way human beings at the top
mock those who are still climbing.

Social Misfit

I had a home
but they treated me
like poverty -
"you make yourself look poor"
an arrow to my chest -
I always felt quite blessed
but perhaps not
without designer labels -

"The things you buy are too simple"
it makes me happy though
"your gifts are not extravagant"
"you don't even have a coat"
oh -
"and we do not like your family"
I am sorry -

I am sorry
I am sorry
I kept saying -
but the biggest apology
is the one I owe to myself
for allowing people
to treat me that way.

Social Misfit

This is an apology to myself
for allowing their words
to become knives
that mocked me for bleeding
while cutting deeper into my skin.

too sensitive

Social Misfit

The ability to feel, to empathise and to understand is a compliment to your character. There are people going through life projecting their insecurities and hurting others, simply because they can barely understand their own feelings. Remember this, the next time someone calls you sensitive.

Social Misfit

I keep the stones they threw
in a glass case
like a trophy collection -
a reminder to celebrate
my heart still beating
despite the kind of attack
that nearly made it stop.

Social Misfit

I spent months wondering why someone would hurt me with words that serrated through my skin. I carry the remnants of their knives with jagged edges on my back. Their echoes of laughter are etched around my clouded memories, the silver linings are stained red, and no matter how much I searched for meaning, I could not understand the reason why they treated me in that way.

Social Misfit

Some words burn
like ash on my tongue -
the pit of my belly remembers
all the pain I swallowed -
starved of kindness
and bleeding from the swords
pulled out of my own back -
I choose to feed on love
now they spit fire at me
forgetting I was once a dragon too.

Social Misfit

The ice in the air
almost spread to my heart -
it could have been carved
into a sculpture of their ideals
if only they had anything
worth believing in -

These were people
without any dreams
asking me to give up on mine -
little did they know
there is warmth in my heart
growing desert flowers -
try to pluck the essence of my being
and you could be poisoned.

Social Misfit

Those without dreams
will never understand the process
of making yours come true.

Social Misfit

It would have been easy to break my seal of kindness, to crack open the swear jar and direct their cruelty back in equal measure, but that is not who I am. I would rather stand at the centre of a warzone without any shield, than attack people who were projecting weakness.

Social Misfit

Scarred and bruised
by words so cruel
it would be easy
to slip into their shoes
and walk down the road
hurting others
the way they do -
but my map
has a different route
and I will not allow
the poisoned bite of their pain
to affect my kindness.

Social Misfit

The thing is, after all the battles I fought without any armour, it was not my scars that provoked them, it was my strength. It took me a long time to realise, but people are intimidated by those who overcome the kind of things they never could. I understand now, that our perception of the world is a reflection of who we are and not what we see. The way we feel about ourselves determines the way we treat other people.

Social Misfit

One must find little value within
to treat another human being
as if they are worth less.

Social Misfit

The daggers in my heart
are imprinted with fingerprints
of the same monsters
living inside of their head.

projection

Social Misfit

Happy people are not cruel -
cruelty is the roaring pain
of a poisoned wound -
like an infection
inside every bitter person -
there is venom soaked
in every insult and opinion -
a projection of what they are feeling

Happy people are kind -
kindness is the essence
of compassion and empathy -
it is like sunlight and water
growing flowers
beneath their ribcage -
every action is a reflection
of this garden blooming within.

Social Misfit

Look for the things that bring out the kindness inside of you, and in your search, there will be cruel people to face, draw your boundaries with a clean sword and walk away. Let them have their opinions, even if they think the worst of you, they might have it all wrong, but that is who they are choosing to be, and only you get to decide who you are.

Part Two
the acceptance

Social Misfit

Social Misfit

Wounds of the wild
unleash stripes
as the tiger prowls
from the murky waters
baring fangs
in a roar of freedom.

Social Misfit

In the heap of my dreams
swept away like dust
there are glittery shards
of hope waiting for a breeze
to find its way back to me.

Social Misfit

There is a painful kind of hope inside of every dreamer that does not allow us to stop, even when we slip and fall from reaching for things out of our sight, with blurred vision and internal bleeding, we stand up somehow, and reach for greater heights.

Social Misfit

Burnt at the stake
like a witch accused of magic -
an unyielding spirit rises
reigniting the pyre
from the ashes of my demise -
the fire cannot consume
those raised in the pits of hell.

rebirth

Social Misfit

Our ghosts dance
in the graveyard
of the mistakes
we made together.

Social Misfit

There are moments we keep
buried in our memories
until a slight remembrance
brings tears - and suddenly
flowers begin to grow.

forget-me-not

Social Misfit

I am no longer the same person -
the pain etched in my memories
has changed me -
there is wisdom in my eyes
that was supposed to arrive
with the first strand of grey hair -
now I am cursed with an understanding
those around me are oblivious to -
gleaming without spectacles.

Social Misfit

Broken mirrors
show the same reflection
of ourselves
in every piece -

A reminder that
even though we lose
parts of our self all the time
we still remain whole.

Social Misfit

The universe speaks through butterflies and flowers, the moon is always talking to the sun, and sometimes, when I eavesdrop on their conversations, it feels like they are talking to me, too.

Social Misfit

The stars talk to me
I feel so little
they say
what do I hope for
when I am going to die anyway -
so we look at each other
curiously in wonder -

My heart beats
as they twinkle
but we both feel the same -
perhaps the purpose of life
is to find our spark
in a great darkness -
for we are more like the stars
than we realise.

Social Misfit

The moon talks
about the darkness
it embraces
like a secret lover -
before light kisses
the crevices
where they hide.

Social Misfit

You stood at the doorstep of my life
in the middle of a storm
and without knocking
you stepped inside -
the sun struck through
like a bolt of lightning
and since that day
you became my lighthouse.

Social Misfit

Loving you
was not enough for your family -
they longed for you to bring home
someone extravagant
to complement the glamour
missing in their lives
and I was too simple -
my good intentions were worth less
than material possessions -
but despite the pity and brutal honesty
that was spat in my face -
my poor broken heart still loved you.

values vs valuables

Social Misfit

These yellow flowers
remind me of the paint
Van Gogh ate -

I pick them for you
wondering whether
it made his portraits
more beautiful
as it killed him -

I pick them for you
wondering whether
loving you
will do the same to me.

Social Misfit

Uprooted from the confines
we were once planted in -
our roots tangle in the soil
nurtured with hope and tears
as we bloom together.

Social Misfit

Lay on the ground next to me
and look up at the sky
we are sunflowers.

Social Misfit

Our love story is poetry that was written
before we learned how to read.

Social Misfit

We broke our hearts
learning how to love each other
but we grasped every piece
and learned how to fix it -
like kintsugi
the japanese art of pottery -
you became the gold
in between my broken pieces.

Social Misfit

He is so gentle with my heart
I could take it out of my chest
 and place it in his hands
 and it will keep beating.

k. h.

Social Misfit

A tangle of sentences
twirl around my tongue
choked by poetry
that makes no sense -

My thoughts dance
off the page in a painting
as my heart sings
with instruments
that sound the way
you make me feel -

In simple words -
I love you.

Social Misfit

You believed in me
when my vision was blurred -
you carried me on your shoulders
and asked me to look for shooting stars
so that you could hear my wishes
and make them come true -
you loved me so much
I started to believe in myself too.

Social Misfit

My tears are watermarks of strength -
I am both soft and strong
and no one can use that against me -
I am the person who cries
and still gets up after the fall.

Social Misfit

My thoughts stain
the walls of my mind
in colours of dolour
like the villains wear
to mask their pain -

In utter darkness
a reflection of light
is enough to make
a twinkle appear
in between our eyes.

meditation

Social Misfit

I am grateful the universe
encapsulates my heart
with kindness and humility
despite the venom of cruelty
seething through snakes that bit me.

healing

Social Misfit

Whispering sacred apologies
to the universe -
the clouds of opinions
that do not belong to me
disappear into the horizon

Energy ripples
like the sky reflects
the ocean's hue
and the clarity attracts
the sun to bloom.

reawakening

Social Misfit

Majestic and misunderstood
the lonesome tiger
emerges from muddy water
like a lotus in bloom
after being shunned
from an internal war
for finding peace within.

serenity

Social Misfit

I whisper thank you
and the universe shouts
here is some more
to be thankful for.

gratitude

Social Misfit

The path exists -
it will take us to our dreams
but the direction
depends on the mileage
we are willing to travel
with only our mind
and a maddening faith
in the road we cannot see.

alignment

Social Misfit

I looked up at the sky today, and something happened. A flock of birds, carrying a string of sound, flew by. It was the missing chord, the reason my heart beat off-key. I felt overwhelmed and excited, was I having an epiphany?

It was somewhat of an awakening, a sudden realization that we travel through clouds and across the sea in search of new scenery, when we can simply look up at the natural palette of colours unravelling each day. And as the birds follow their instinct, we will find our way.

Social Misfit

I am still healing
the pain has not disappeared -
like salt dissolving in water
I can no longer see it
but I still remember the taste.

Social Misfit

History does not hide
the generations of women
who like me were treated
as if dignity was dependent
on the absence of melanin -
our skin was too dark
to deserve any respect

Shamed for being born
below the standard of beauty -
we were cast out and criticised
because being wrapped
in the colour of the earth
meant our blood carried dirt

We bared the brunt of taunts
for our bronzed knees
while our cousins were worshipped
for their rosy cheeks -
we were silenced in attempt to speak
learning brown skin was not for the weak

It took centuries of women
who stood gracefully -
burning in the sunlight
to challenge the irony
and change the narrative
for us to embrace our glow.

Social Misfit

My skin is the colour of soil
it deepens in the warm embrace of the sun
and glows in the same light

My roots tangle with the earth
as flowers grow in my untamed hair
bees follow and pollen glistens around me

Golden hues reflect in my aura
like the energy of a goddess
existing in oneness with nature.

Social Misfit

Stolen from their land
my ancestors bravely
traveled across the sea
so that I could be -

Born into a rainbow nation
rich in culture and diversity
their struggle and resilience
reminisced in history books
became an epitome of my being -

The lamp in my home
ignites my spirit
with an inexplicable feeling
the same one I get
when my grandmother ties
a saree around me -

My heart beats
to the sound of a tabla
and my mind wanders to
my heritage across the sea
I am at home but -
India still calls out to me.

heritage beyond home

Social Misfit

My tea keeps getting cold
before I could drink it -
my mind wanders away
as the cup sits on the counter
waiting for me -
life happens similarly.

my youth is fleeting

Social Misfit

Wildflowers grow
through my chest -
they stick out my ears
and cover my eyes
each time someone
is unkind to me -

It appears to be weeds
perhaps that is why
it keeps happening -
but beneath the surface
I am simply a garden
becoming a grave.

Social Misfit

We do not have forever
eventually our time will stop
while the clocks keep ticking
we will walk out the last door
leaving behind everything

This house will still be a home
but for someone else
that car will eventually rust
like the memories
of the clothes we wore

No one will remember then
the things that matter now
and all we worried about
will become as worthless
as the things we kept dying for.

Social Misfit

My heart stopped beating
but I feel more alive
than the living

My success is buried
with the dreams I once had
and goals out of my reach

Staring at my cold body
their disappointment
is warped into admiration

Nobody remembers
my paycheck
or the price I paid to survive

But the kindness
of my heart still beats
in fading memories.

poem from the dead

Social Misfit

To live in this world
we must bring alive
the dead poets
immortality to survive.

Social Misfit

It took years to build this mind palace
from cardboard boxes to steady bricks
remembering the value my thoughts carry -
despite the splinters of insecurity

There are ghosts hiding in the shreds
of the crumpled paper walls
they wear like sheets to frighten me -
but fear no longer exists here

Wandering through the corridors
where old beliefs linger in longing
like books waiting for a reader -
not all stories are written to be told

Stepping outside to a garden of possibility
the castle begins to disappear
swallowed by smoke and mirrors -
my dreams are free to roam.

freedom

The choices we make create the path we take, there will always be forks in the middle of the road and we will have no choice but to choose, often without any knowledge of what lies ahead, but this is what separates the dreamers from those without any dreams. Those who believe they have what it takes to bring their imagination to life, know it does not matter which path you take, as long as you don't follow those with a rule book and directions to the same place.

Social Misfit

There is a silent hunt
in the fiery eyes of a tiger
who escaped the cage
like a declawed kitten
to live in the jungle of solitude.

social misfit

Social Misfit

ABOUT THE AUTHOR

Ekta Somera is a South African youth activist, author, and founder of Paper Trail Literary Journal. She was named among the Mail & Guardian 200 Young South Africans in 2022. Ekta plays a significant role in advocating for policy changes to combat youth unemployment in South Africa, and she brings dreams to life through her career at a book publishing company. Ekta lives by the words of Jim Carrey: "You can fail at what you don't want, so you might as well take a chance on doing what you love."

In her third collection of poetry, "Social Misfit," Ekta Somera delivers a riveting collection of prose that captivates readers with a sense of effortless creation as if each poem emerged spontaneously from the whispers of the universe. The verses carry the weight of her tender youth and the harsh realities she has faced, revealing resilience and vulnerability. Ekta's poetic storytelling transcends her intricate thoughts and memories, reflecting a journey of healing and self-discovery. Through her words, she navigates the complexities of her experiences, ultimately finding a way to release them and embrace a new beginning. Each piece invites readers to join her in exploring beauty, pain, and the profound act of letting go.

The collection is thoughtfully divided into two parts, "the rejection" and "the acceptance," mirroring the emotional journey that the poems undertake. Somera's use of vivid metaphors and imagery adds richness to the work, as she skillfully compares words to knives and the heart to a garden, conveying the intricate emotions and experiences that define us.

Throughout the collection, Somera tackles significant themes with sensitivity and nuance, including the impact of words, the search for belonging, the pain of judgment, and the transformative power of self-love. Her exploration of heritage and identity adds a valuable layer of depth and cultural richness to the work.

One of the most striking aspects of Somera's style is its deceptive simplicity, which belies a profound emotional intelligence and a mastery of evocative language. The poems are powerful and relatable, offering readers a journey of self-discovery and healing that is deeply personal and universally resonant. Ultimately, "Social Misfit" is a moving and insightful collection offering a profound and enduring reflection on the human condition.

– **James N. McManus** *(Poet and Author of Travels a Poetic Journey, Poetry from Afar, and A Glimpse of Me - a Book of Poetic Thoughts)*

Social Misfit

www.ingramcontent.com/pod-product-compliance
Lightning Source LLC
LaVergne TN
LVHW021120080426
835510LV00012B/1771